LEE EVANS ARRANGES

ANTONIO CARLOS JOBIM

PIANO SOLOS

CONTENTS

To Kelly Welles

Cover photo by: Ana Lontra Jobim
Cover photo handpainted by: James Foster-Levy

Hal Leonard Publishing Corporation

7777 West Bluemound Road P.O. Box 13819 Milwaukee, WI 53213

LOOK TO THE SKY

By ANTONIO CARLOS JOBIM

Arranged by LEE EVANS

Slow Bossa Nova (♩ = 108)

LAMENTO

Words by VINICIUS DE MORAES
Music by ANTONIO CARLOS JOBIM
Arranged by LEE EVANS

Bright Bossa Nova (= 104)

WAVE

By ANTONIO CARLOS JOBIM
Arranged by LEE EVANS

Bright Bossa Nova (♩ = 80)

ANTIGUA

By ANTONIO CARLOS JOBIM
Arranged by LEE EVANS

Medium Bossa Nova (♩ = 144)

THE RED BLOUSE

By ANTONIO CARLOS JOBIM
Arranged by LEE EVANS

Bright Bossa Nova ($\quad$ = 88)

(No pedal throughout)

To Coda

D.S. al Coda
with repeat

CODA

8va

gliss.

sfz

(loco)

*Start gliss. on 1st beat (with 3rd and 4th R.H. fingers.)

QUIET NIGHTS OF QUIET STARS
(CORCOVADO)

English Words by GENE LEES
Original Words & Music by ANTONIO CARLOS JOBIM
Arranged by LEE EVANS

Gently, in a steady tempo ($\quarternote$ = 126)

32

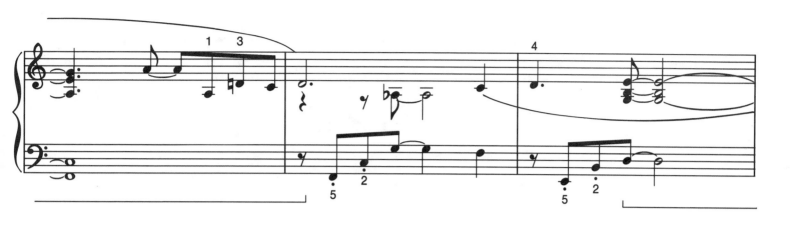

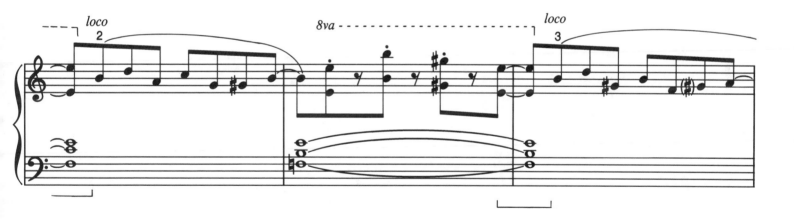

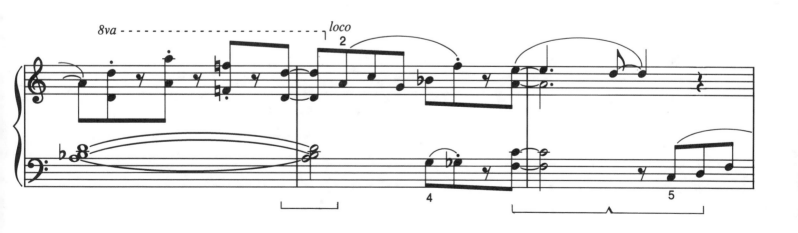

THE GIRL FROM IPANEMA
(GAROTA DE IPANEMA)

Original Words by VINICIUS DE MORAES
English Words by NORMAN GIMBEL
Music by ANTONIO CARLOS JOBIM
Arranged by LEE EVANS

Bossa Nova; playfully (♩ = 92)

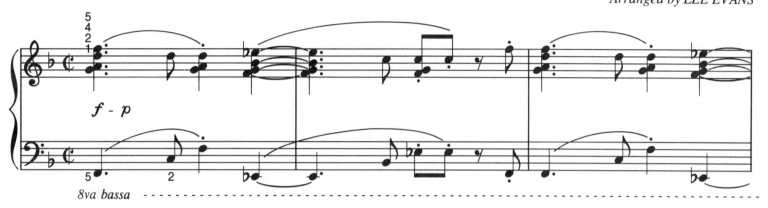

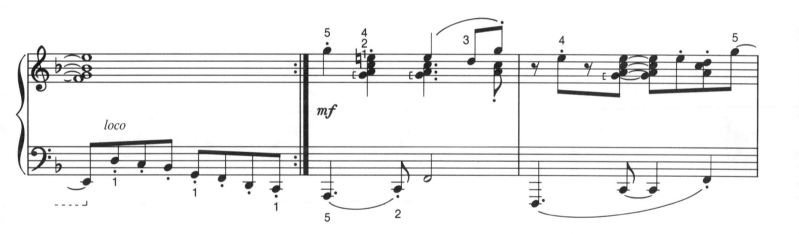

Ped.

poco a poco cresc.

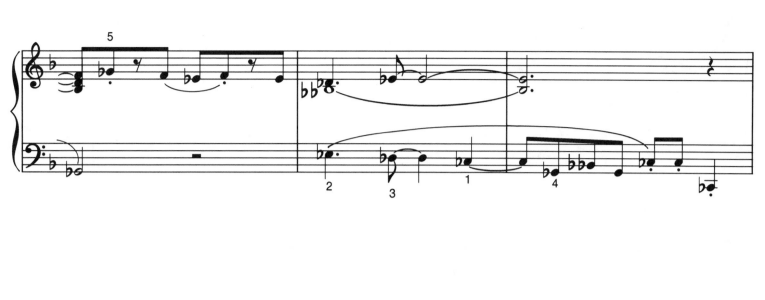

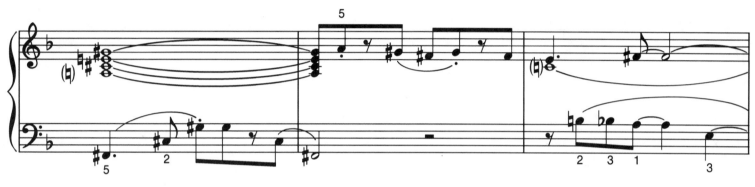

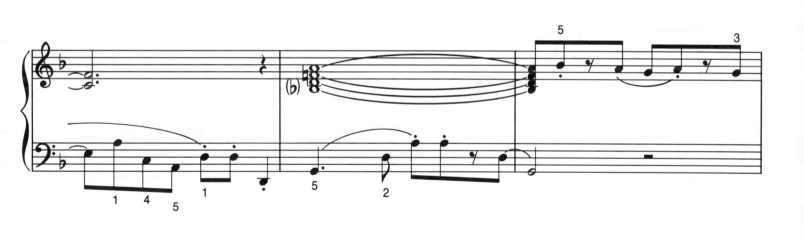

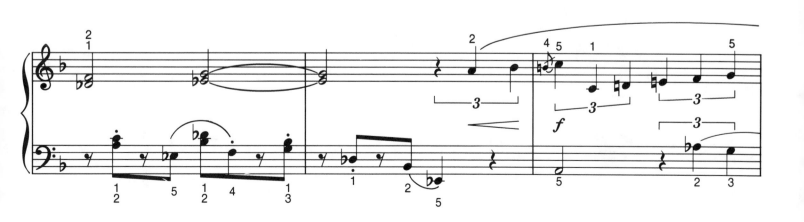

42

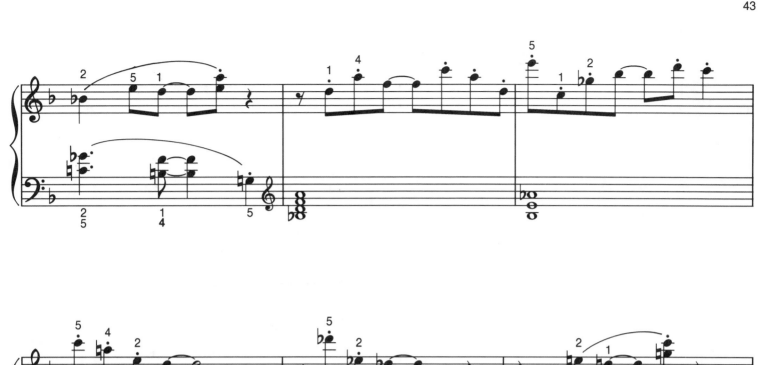

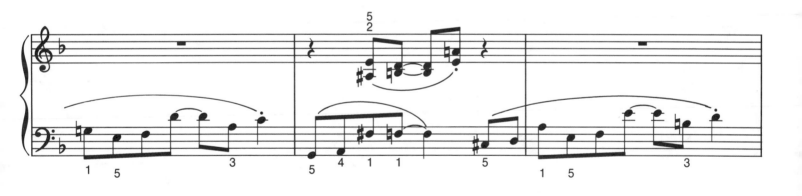

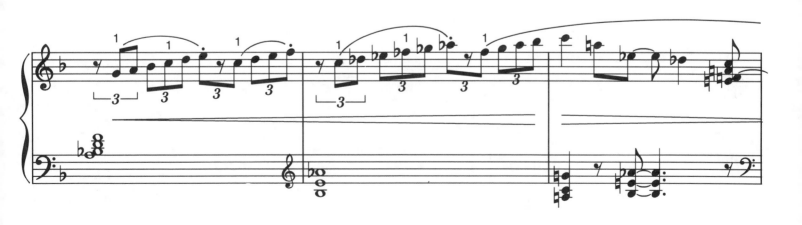

44

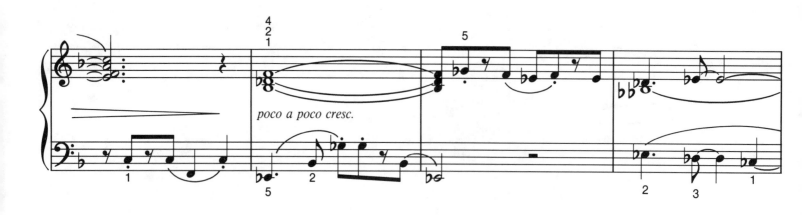

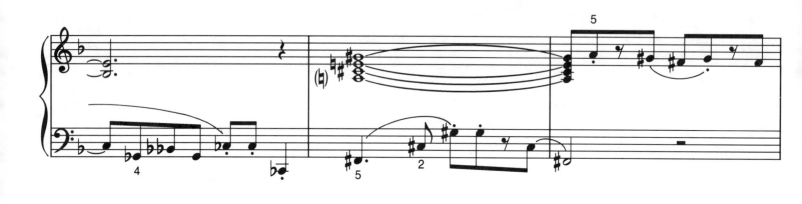

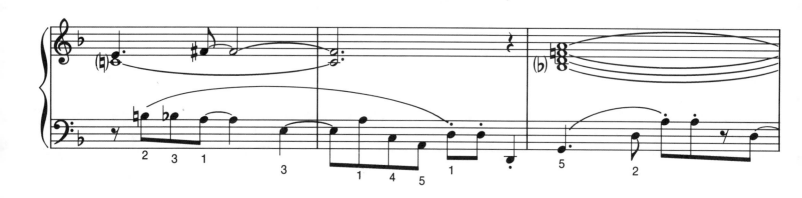

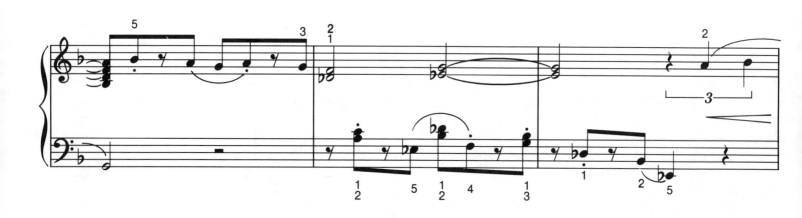

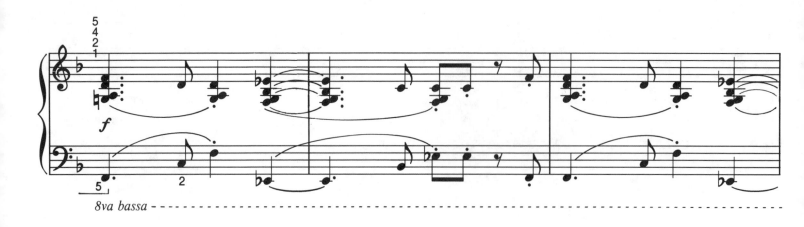

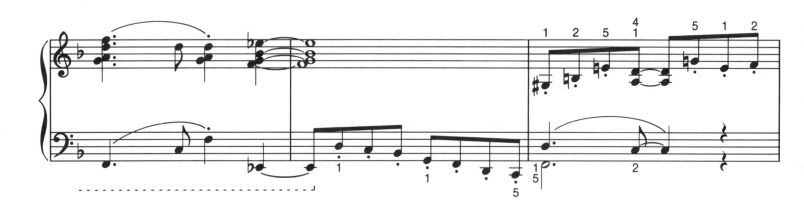

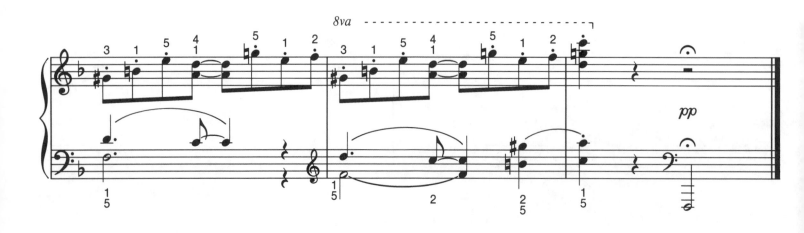

TRISTE

By ANTONIO CARLOS JOBIM
Arranged by LEE EVANS

Bright Bossa Nova (♩ = 104)

56

SONG OF THE SABIA

English Words by NORMAN GIMBEL
Music by ANTONIO CARLOS JOBIM
Arranged by LEE EVANS

DESAFINADO
(SLIGHTLY OUT OF TUNE)

English Words by JON HENDRICKS & JESSIE CAVANAUGH
Original Words by NEWTON MENDONCA
Music by ANTONIO CARLOS JOBIM
Arranged by LEE EVANS

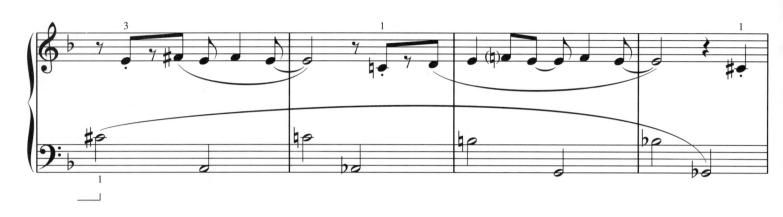

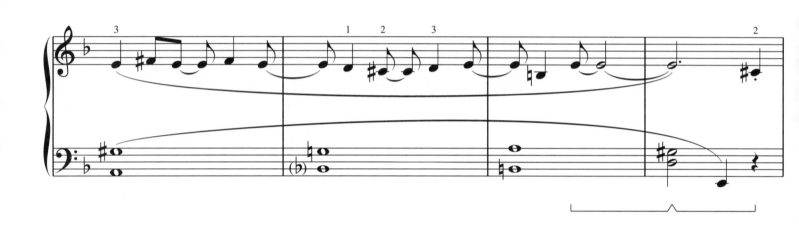

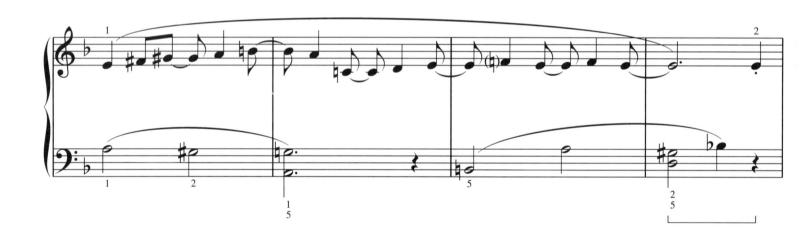

69

SE TODOS FOSSEM IGUAIS A VOCE
(Someone To Light Up My Life)

Original Text by VINICIUS DE MORAES
Music by ANTONIO CARLOS JOBIM
Arranged by LEE EVANS

(Chorus)

74

MOJAVE

By ANTONIO CARLOS JOBIM
Arranged by LEE EVANS

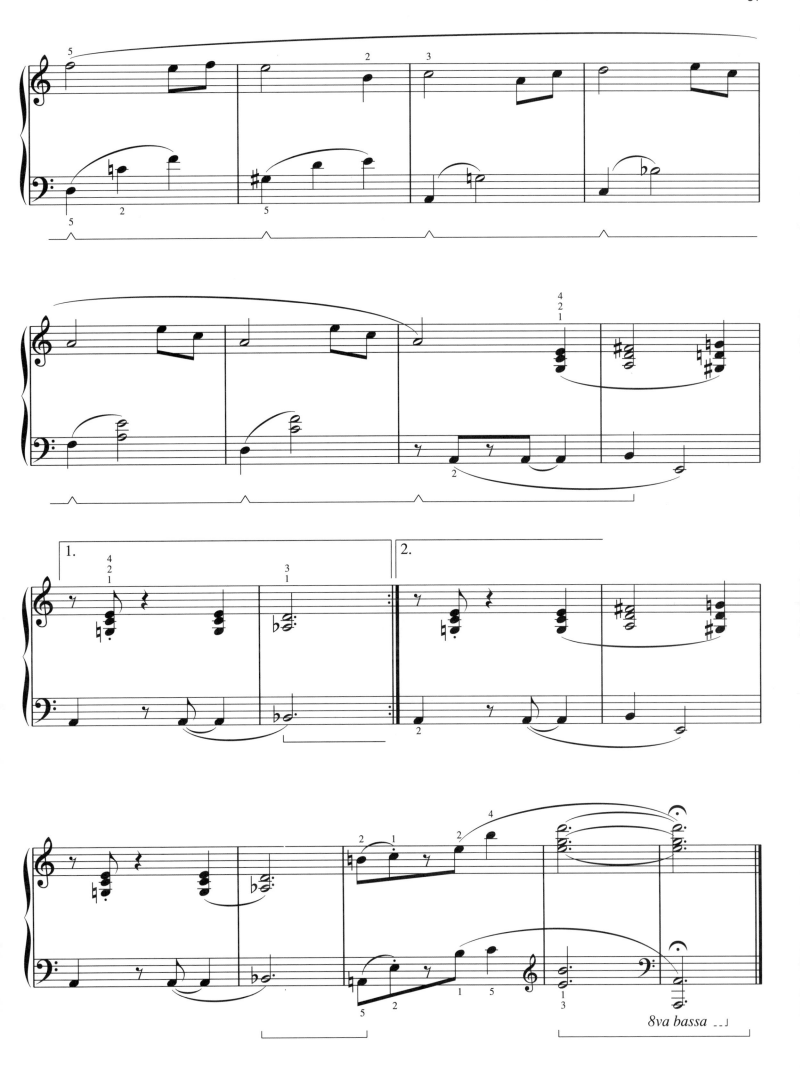

SO DANCO SAMBA
(JAZZ 'N' SAMBA)
From the film "COPACABANA PALACE"

Words and Music by VINICIUS DE MORAES
and ANTONIO CARLOS JOBIM
Arranged by LEE EVANS

Slow Samba or Bright Bossa Nova; Leggiero

CHEGA DE SAUDADE
(No More Blues)

Words by VINICIUS DE MORAES
Music by ANTONIO CARLOS JOBIM
Arranged by LEE EVANS

portato

poco a poco cresc.

SAMBA DO AVAIO
(Song Of The Jet)

Words and Music by
ANTONIO CARLOS JOBIM
Arranged by LEE EVANS

MEDITATION

English Words by NORMAN GIMBEL
Original Words by NEWTON MENDONCA
Music by ANTONIO CARLOS JOBIM
Arranged by LEE EVANS

Bossa Nova; *leggiero* (♩ = 144)

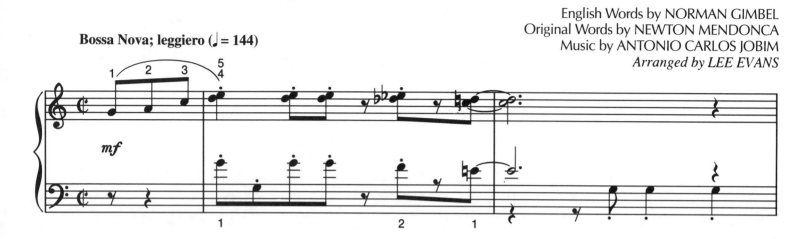

*A broken phrase sign offers visual logic
to a phrase containing rests or staccato marks.

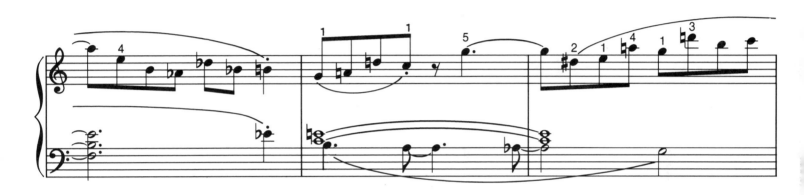